NATIONAL
GEOGRAPHIC

A Tree's Life

David Tunkin

A pine tree grows in the forest.
It grows big and tall and strong.
Where did the pine tree come from?

A pine tree starts as a seedling.
The seedling grows from pine tree
seeds that have fallen on the ground.

The seedling grows bigger and taller.

After two years this little pine tree
is called a sapling.

The sapling grows into a pine tree.
The pine tree grows year after year.
After 25 years it is big and tall and strong.

Pinecones grow on the pine tree.
Inside the pinecones are seeds.
The seeds fall to the ground.

11

Little seedlings grow.